RED

By AMANDA DOERING

Illustrations by RONNY GAZZOLA

Music by MARK OBLINGER

CANTATA
LEARNING

WWW.CANTATALEARNING.COM

CANTATA LEARNING

Published by Cantata Learning
1710 Roe Crest Drive
North Mankato, MN 56003
www.cantatalearning.com

Library of Congress Cataloging-in-Publication Data

Names: Doering, Amanda F., 1980– author. | Gazzola, Ronny, illustrator. |
 Oblinger, Mark, composer.
Title: Red / by Amanda Doering ; illustrated by Ronny Gazzola ; music by Mark
 Oblinger.
Description: North Mankato, MN : Cantata Learning, [2018] | Series: Sing your
 colors! | Audience: Ages 4–7. | Audience: K to grade 3. | Includes lyrics
 and sheet music. | Includes bibliographical references.
Identifiers: LCCN 2017017521 (print) | LCCN 2017038292 (ebook) | ISBN
 9781684101702 (ebook) | ISBN 9781684101283 (hardcover : alk. paper) | ISBN
 9781684102013 (pbk. : alk. paper)
Subjects: LCSH: Red--Juvenile literature. | Colors--Juvenile literature. |
 Children's songs, English.
Classification: LCC QC495.5 (ebook) | LCC QC495.5 .D6445 2018 (print) | DDC
 535.6--dc23
LC record available at https://lccn.loc.gov/2017017521

Book design and art direction, Tim Palin Creative
Editorial direction, Kellie M. Hultgren
Music direction, Elizabeth Draper
Music arranged and produced by Mark Oblinger

Printed in the United States of America in North Mankato, Minnesota.
122017   0378CGS18

ACCESS THE MUSIC!

SCAN CODE WITH MOBILE APP

CANTATALEARNING.COM

TIPS TO SUPPORT LITERACY AT HOME

WHY READING AND SINGING WITH YOUR CHILD IS SO IMPORTANT

Daily reading with your child leads to increased academic achievement. Music and songs, specifically rhyming songs, are a fun and easy way to build early literacy and language development. Music skills correlate significantly with both phonological awareness and reading development. Singing helps build vocabulary and speech development. And reading and appreciating music together is a wonderful way to strengthen your relationship.

READ AND SING EVERY DAY!

TIPS FOR USING CANTATA LEARNING BOOKS AND SONGS DURING YOUR DAILY STORY TIME

1. As you sing and read, point out the different words on the page that rhyme. Suggest other words that rhyme.

2. Memorize simple rhymes such as Itsy Bitsy Spider and sing them together. This encourages comprehension skills and early literacy skills.

3. Use the questions in the back of each book to guide your singing and storytelling.

4. Read the included sheet music with your child while you listen to the song. How do the music notes correlate to the words of the song?

5. Sing along on the go and at home. Access music by scanning the QR code on each Cantata book, or by using the included CD. You can also stream or download the music for free to your computer, smartphone, or mobile device.

Devoting time to daily reading shows that you are available for your child. Together, you are building language, literacy, and listening skills.

Have fun reading and singing!

Red is a **primary color**. It is mixed with other primary colors to make **secondary colors**. Red mixed with blue makes purple. Red mixed with yellow makes orange. But you cannot mix other colors to make red. That is what makes primary colors so special.

Red is a **warm color** that makes us feel excited. Turn the page to learn all about red things and where they can be found!

Red is hot. Red is sweet.

You can wear red on your feet.

8

Red can tell us when to stop.

We find red signs when we shop.

Where is red?
Here and there.

Where is red?
Everywhere!

11

Red can help put out a fire.

Red can sit upon a wire.

Red is fun to use in art.

Red looks great on a heart.

Where is red?
Here and there.

Where is red?
Everywhere!

Red can grow up from the ground.
We find red all around!

Where is red?
Here and there.

Where is red?
Everywhere!

Red is everywhere!

SONG LYRICS
Red

Red is hot. Red is sweet.
You can wear red on your feet.

Red can tell us when to stop.
We find red signs when we shop.

Where is red?
Here and there.
Where is red?
Everywhere!

Red can help put out a fire.
Red can sit upon a wire.

Red is fun to use in art.
Red looks great on a heart.

Where is red?
Here and there.
Where is red?
Everywhere!

Red can grow up from the ground.
We find red all around!

Where is red?
Here and there.
Where is red?
Everywhere!
Red is everywhere!

Red

Latin Jazz
Mark Oblinger

Verse

1. Red is hot. Red is sweet. You can wear red on your feet.

Verse 2
Red can tell us when to stop.
We find red signs when we shop.

Chorus

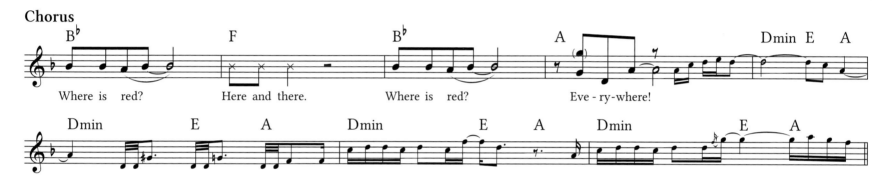

Where is red? Here and there. Where is red? Eve-ry-where!

Verse 3
Red can help put out a fire.
Red can sit upon a wire.

Verse 4
Red is fun to use in art.
Red looks great on a heart.

Chorus

Verse 5
Red can grow up from the ground.
We find red all around!

Outro

Where is red? Here and there. Where is red? Eve-ry-where! Red is eve-ry-where!

GLOSSARY

primary colors—colors, such as blue, red, and yellow, mixed to make other colors

secondary colors—colors, such as orange, green, and purple, made by mixing two primary colors

warm color—a bold and exciting color that we see in nature, such as red, yellow, and orange.

GUIDED READING ACTIVITIES

1. What red things do you see in the pictures of this book? Can you find the following things: a poppy (a type of flower), a cardinal (a type of bird), a strawberry, a pepper, and a stop sign?

2. Sometimes colors make us feel a certain way. What do you feel when you see red? Why do you think you feel that way?

3. Using crayons or markers, draw your favorite red thing. Is there anything red that you do not like? If so, draw that, too.

TO LEARN MORE

Borth, Teddy. *Red Animals*. Minneapolis: Abdo Kids, 2015.

Ghigna, Charles. *The Wonders of the Color Wheel*. North Mankato, MN: Capstone, 2014.

Rustad, Martha E. H. *Red Foods*. North Mankato, MN: Capstone, 2017.

Shores, Erika L. *Fall Leaves*. North Mankato, MN: Capstone, 2016.